The Plant-based Diet

A Christian Option?

Mia Smith

Chaplain of Hertford College, Oxford

GROVE BOOKS LIMITED
RIDLEY HALL RD CAMBRIDGE CB3 9HU

Contents

1 The Plant-based Diet—A Christian Option? 3

2 Our Choices and Other Creatures—A Non-violent Option?........6

3 Our Choices and Ourselves—A Healthy Option? 11

4 Our Choices and the Earth—A Sustainable Option?.................14

5 Our Choices and the Global Population—
  An Equitable Option?...19

6 The Plant-based Diet—A Viable Christian Option?..................22

  Notes 26

Acknowledgments
With thanks to students and colleagues at Hertford College for sharing their thoughts, and to my resident vegans and flexitarians for their support and example.

First Impression July 2019
ISSN 1470–854X
ISBN 978 1 78827 090 8

The Plant-based Diet—
A Christian Option?[1]

On 3 January 2019, a new product hit the British high street. It sold out almost immediately, precipitating a nationwide launch and extensive media attention. The company was bakery giant, Greggs, and the product was the vegan sausage roll. Within weeks, Greggs' sales had increased by almost ten per cent, and annual sales broke through the £1 billion barrier for the first time.[2]

That Greggs, famed for sausage rolls and cheese pasties, would launch a vegan product might have seemed impossible until recently and, while veganism may not (yet?) be entirely mainstream, it is rapidly becoming more acceptable. In 2018 the UK launched the highest number of new vegan food products in Europe, with one in six food products launched being vegan-friendly. One in four household evening meals in the UK is meat free, and fifty-six per cent of consumers adopt vegan buying behaviours.[3] This increased vegan activity highlights popular concern about animal welfare, the environment and what constitutes a healthy diet.

How, therefore, might Christians best respond to this growing trend? Is eating animal products problematic to our faith? Might there be an ethical and theological case for the plant-based diet to be considered a legitimately Christian option?

Opinions for and against the plant-based diet are plentiful, particularly across social media. In an atmosphere of fake news, virtue signalling and echo chambers, it is difficult to know where the facts lie. This booklet explores reliable sources of information (mostly from recent scientific studies in high-impact factor publications) thus enabling readers to decide for themselves how a plant-based diet might affect animal welfare, human health and the environment. A case will be made for theological engagement with each of these issues as part of Christian discipleship.

It is my hope that this booklet will assist the reader in making strong dietary choices which will enable our fellow humans, non-human creatures and the environment to be fully what God created them to be. Questions at the end of each chapter are provided to stimulate personal reflection on the subject matter.

The Human Vocation and the Concerns of Veganism

The questions raised by veganism are essentially theological concerns, rising out of the human vocation: our God-given duty towards our fellow creatures, one another and the planet. Before we examine each concern, we need to explore our human vocation to understand why our diet is theologically significant.

The starting point is this: our species belongs to creation. We are not to God's benefit, and we add nothing to his nature. We are creatures, having more in common with our non-human fellow creatures than we do with the creator. God's loving purposes encompass the whole of creation, not just the human creature.

John 3.16 states, 'God so loved the world (Greek *kosmos*) that he gave his only Son, so that everyone (Greek *pas*) who believes in him may not perish but may have eternal life.'[4] Notice two words here: 'world' and 'everyone.' First, world (*kosmos*)—God's love is not limited to humanity, but is cosmic. Secondly, everyone (*pas*) who believes may have eternal life. *Pas* is also used in Col 1.20, God reconciling 'all things' to himself.[5] *Pas*, therefore, is broad in scope, encompassing both any and everyone, and any and every kind. Reconciliation is not limited to human creatures, but extends to the whole of creation. 2 Cor 5.19 reminds us of our role: 'In Christ God was reconciling the world to himself…and entrusting the message of reconciliation to us.'

We are not told in the creation narratives *why* God created, but it is clear throughout Scripture that the whole of creation, humanity included, is meant to bring joy, and to reflect praise back to God. So what, if anything, is distinctive about humanity?

The first creation narrative (Gen 1.26–28) emphasizes the connection between humanity and the divine, and the second (Gen 2.4–25) the connection between humanity and the earth. We are part of creation, sharing its nature and its fate. Yet of that creation we are summoned (alone among the creatures) to bear the divine image as a 'reflection of God within creation.'[6] Much ink has been spilled on what it might mean to be made in God's image. Graham Tomlin helpfully argues that God's image might primarily be found not so much in human attributes but in this distinct calling in creation to develop and to keep it from harm:[7]

> Be fruitful and multiply, and fill the earth and subdue it; and have dominion over the fish of the sea and over the birds of the air and over every living thing that moves upon the earth. (Gen 1.28)

This text does not imply that dominion *is* the image but 'a *consequence* of humanity's being in God's image,' expressed in peace and flourishing, as a steward and partner, not as exploitation.[8] The creation narratives imply that the responsibility to protect creation is not primarily a Christian calling, but lies with the whole human species:

> ...through protecting creation from harm, humanity helps bring the divine blessing, the movement of creation towards its renewal and fulfilment.[9]

The tragedy is that humanity, despite a vocation to prevent damage and chaos in creation, has been the agent of hastening its destruction. It is here that Christians have a specific calling. As Basil the Great reminds us, although we are *made* in God's *image*, we need to *grow* into his *likeness*,[10] and the distinctive calling of the church in creation is to develop and protect people, to remind humanity what it has the potential to be.[11] The church is called to remind humanity of its purpose and end, that 'Creation itself will be liberated from its bondage to decay and brought into the freedom and glory of the children of God' (Rom 8.21). We are called out of humanity to bear witness to God's intention to reconcile all things to himself in Christ (Col 1.20), and to be entrusted with the message of reconciliation (2 Cor 5.19). The church is therefore ideally placed to bear prophetic witness to the reconciliation of all things by identification with issues of planetary, creaturely and human well-being.

Therefore it is a legitimately Christian task to examine our actions and choices in view of our dual vocations as human creatures and as the people of God, as we seek to grow into Christ's likeness.

It is in this consideration of the human vocation that Christian theology intersects with the concerns of veganism. Many people who identify as vegan do so because they identify with concerns for animal welfare or the environment. Others identify with a growing body of evidence to do with human health. These concerns will be examined in turn in the coming chapters.

2   Our Choices and Other Creatures—A Non-violent Option?

It is 6am. A small group of humans huddles together by the roadside, wrapped up against the winter cold. A vehicle approaches. One of the humans gestures a peace sign to the driver. The vehicle slows down, and the group approaches. Pushing water bottles through gaps, they offer both drinks and reassurances to the occupants, a drove of frightened pigs. It is a tender moment, creature to creature. Then the vehicle continues its journey through the gates of the abattoir.

This is a deeply prophetic snapshot. Members of Animal Saves, who show kindness to animals on their final journey are, unwittingly or otherwise, bearing witness to the new creation, in which there will be no more death or crying or pain (Rev 21.4).

It is an uncomfortable fact that modern food production contributes to previously unimaginable creaturely suffering. In this chapter I will argue that there is a great discrepancy between God's purposes for animals and how we treat them. I will go on to suggest that there are good reasons, both theological and scientific, for narrowing, or even eliminating, that chasm.

God's Purpose for Non-Human Creatures

Creation is an act of grace on the part of the creator, both for creation's sake, and so that creation may glorify God. Creation is theocentric, and no one creature exists solely for the flourishing of another. Basil the Great stated that there were no creaturely degrees of being; everything created has the same ontological status. There is God, and there are creatures, and humanity is of the second kind, the 'creaturekind.'[12] The whole of creation, not just humanity, is declared to be good by the creator, and creatures of all kinds depend on him and on the rest of creation (Gen 1.25).

The Old Testament frequently uses pastoral imagery in describing God's loving kindness. This imagery was adopted by Jesus, for example in his claim, 'I am the good shepherd. The good shepherd lays down his life for the sheep' (John 10.11). This is contrasted with the exploitation of animals by those who wish to steal, kill or destroy. The Parable of the Lost Sheep also demonstrates concern for the welfare of animals (Luke 15). Jesus suggests that humanity may have something to learn from non-humans; for example, unlike humans, birds do not worry about food, yet God takes care of them (Luke 12). Pope Francis emphasized this in his encyclical *Laudato Si'*:[13]

> Every creature is…the object of the Father's tenderness, who gives it its place in the world. Even the fleeting life of the least of beings is the object of his love.

Not only does the doctrine of *creation* indicate that creatures matter, but so does the doctrine of *reconciliation*, as discussed in the introduction. The word became flesh; that is, Jesus was born as a mammalian creature, in order to redeem the whole of creation. With the rest of creation, we look ahead to the future harmony of a redeemed creation, when all creatures worship together (Rev 5.13):

> Then I heard every creature in heaven and on earth and under the earth and in the sea, and all that is in them, singing, 'To the one seated on the throne and to the Lamb be blessing and honour and glory and might forever and ever!'

Animal suffering is therefore problematic to Christians, both because God loves and will redeem creation, and because cruelty diminishes God's image in us.[14] Animals belong to God, Karl Barth claimed, not to humans, and God requires an accounting of every animal killed for food (Gen 9.5). Barth recognized the ethical importance of animal welfare, stating that we must be 'careful, considerate, friendly, and above all, understanding' in our treatment of other creatures.[15] The killing of animals for food should, Barth claims, only be done out of necessity, otherwise it is murder.

Once we begin to take seriously that God wants the whole of creation to thrive, then the need to respect our fellow creatures gains traction. How animals both live and die matters to God.

Our Treatment of Non-Human Creatures

A tradition of anthropocentricism has led to a common axiom that creation's reason for existence is to serve humanity. Many theologians throughout history have supported this, which has led to criticism from ethicists such as Peter Singer, who accuses Christianity of speciesism, that is, claiming humanity's superiority of one species over another. Jesus stated that the one who wished to be great must be like the 'one who serves' (Luke 22.27). The correct interpretation of dominion is not exploitation, but rather it reflects the loving service God exercises towards creation. It involves 'respect, protection and care' rather than 'mastery and manipulation.'[16] Humanity's essential self in contrast to non-rational creatures does not make us superior; it makes us responsible to treat them with dignity.

The intensification of farmed animal production has increased over the past two hundred years, especially escalating since the middle of the twentieth century. In his article, 'Consuming Animal Creatures,' David Clough presents a number of distressing snapshots of the lives and deaths for which the contemporary human food industry is responsible.[17]

- A large percentage of animals killed for food are fish, with huge collateral damage to non-targeted species.[18]

- Virtually all egg production (including organic and free range) involves the sexing of chicks at hatching, with a cull of males. Annually, over four billion chicks are killed globally, usually by maceration.

- Chickens make up around one in three animals killed for food. Many broiler hens reach slaughter weight by about thirty-five days, often living their entire lives in warehouses with artificial light. Broiler chickens are bred in such a way that their body weight is too great for their joints, causing constant pain, so painkillers are added to the food. [19]

- Most pigs are kept in monotonous and crowded indoor sheds with slatted floors for their whole lives, with no room to turn round.

- Most dairy calves are taken from their mothers before they suckle for the first time, forcing mothers to produce at rates which require unnatural feeding. A significant proportion of these are kept indoors permanently, without having the opportunity to graze grass, and are culled for beef once their yields begin to drop.

- Most beef cattle and sheep are raised intensively, and although they fare better than cows and chickens, they are slaughtered at around six months, with no opportunity to grow to maturity. They are often subject to painful procedures, such as branding and castration, without anaesthetic.

Utilitarian ethicists such as Singer argue that the capacity of a creature to suffer (and not necessarily to reason) confers rights on that creature. Scientists agree that animal rights should be based on sentience, rather than a creature's capacity to reason (as definitions of animal consciousness are still elusive).[20] The snapshots highlight the creaturely capacity for suffering, and Clough concludes, therefore, that 'The vast majority of animal products currently offered for sale should be off the table for Christians.'[21]

Closing the Gap

We live in a fallen creation, and acknowledge that we are far away from the peaceable kingdom where predation is ended and creatures live in peace (Isa 11.6–8). To save prey from predators would cause suffering in itself. We therefore look forward to the liberation of creation. However, in the meantime we can make choices which relieve the suffering we have inflicted on fellow creatures through the cruelty of intensive farming.

David Ferguson states that evolutionary science has increased humanity's kinship with animals by highlighting our common ancestral origins.[22] He argues that we have a growing sense of divine purpose expressed in ethical awareness, resulting in campaigns surrounding living or slaughter conditions for livestock, or our response to the threat of extinction of species.

Even where animal suffering is not a priority for consumers, animal scientist Marian Dawkins argues that their welfare is essential because of human self-interest.[23]

Seventy-five per cent of new diseases in humans over the past decade have originated from animals or animal products. In addition, antibiotic use in livestock is promoting resistance in humans. In a review of 139 academic studies, only seven (five per cent) argued that there was no link between livestock antibiotics and resistance in humans, while 100 (72 per cent) found such evidence.[24] This demonstrates that animal and human welfare are intimately connected. The well-being of animals is not a luxury, but part of a multidisciplinary effort to fight human disease.

Antibiotic use in livestock is promoting resistance in humans

Efforts to ensure that animals are treated in line with their indicated preferences enhances their well-being and therefore reduces disease. Her study calculating the floor space used by chickens with free movement, then comparing them with the space offered in battery cages, showed that they were unable to act naturally. Chickens were willing to perform undesirable tasks in order to gain more space. Animal welfare, she states, must not be drowned out by calls for increased production.[25]

Similarly, a study of pigs from intensive systems who were placed in varied parkland found that they began to build communal nests and shelters, allocated separate toilet and eating areas, and built complex social relationships. Their behaviours began to resemble those of their wild boar ancestors. Both studies show how chickens and pigs might begin to flourish, and in doing so, glorify their creator.[26]

Culture, tradition and taste all inform our dietary choices, and reconsidering our habits is always challenging. Yet in order to bridge the gap between modern animal product consumption and God's purposes for his creatures we need to make changes in our diets, either by sourcing ethical goods, or by eliminating animal products from our diets.

Christians should therefore avoid participating in food systems which prevent flourishing. There are strong arguments for following a vegan or vegetarian diet, as a protest and a prophetic choice. Christians may, of course, disagree about the elimination of animal-based products as a faith-based obligation. As Clough argues, 'The perfect seems to be the enemy of the better in this area of ethics.'[27] Others may prefer, instead, simply to buy products from farming systems which do not make us feel ashamed, especially by rejecting factory farming, or to consume less frequently, as a treat rather than as a staple. If we do make use of animals for food, then it must be uncontroversial to argue that we should ensure that our use of animal-based food respects their status as our fellow creatures of God.

Questions for Reflection

- How much do I know about the origins of my food?

- How important an issue is animal welfare for me?

Our Choices and Ourselves—
A Healthy Option?

3

A theological and scientific case has been made for Christians to consider the exclusion or reduction of animal dietary products on the basis of animal well-being. So how does a plant-based diet contribute to human health and well-being? Does prioritizing animal well-being put our own health at risk? Might it even be possible to have a healthier diet without meat or dairy products?

Why Think about Diet?

The Bible indicates that care of our own health is important if we are to fulfil our human vocation, indicating that, as the body is a temple of the Holy Spirit, God should be glorified in our bodies (1 Cor 6.19–20). We are permitted to eat all foods, but not all foods are beneficial (1 Cor 10.23), and whatever we eat or drink should be to the glory of God, as part of a life of worship (v 31).

In speaking about household relationships, Eph 5.29 states that, 'No-one ever hates his own body, but he nourishes and tenderly cares for it, just as Christ does for the church.' This example of an ideal is interesting, given that we do not always care for and nurture our bodies well. Whatever we choose to eat, the Christian needs to be mindful of the significance of those choices and the risks and benefits that they involve. The reduction of foods which may be harmful, and their replacement with foods which have proven nutritional benefits, is part of our discipleship, ensuring that we, along with others, thrive.

A recent study in *The Lancet* showed that suboptimal diet is an important risk factor for non-communicable diseases and, by evaluating the consumption of major foods and nutrients across 195 countries, quantified the impact of suboptimal nutrition.[28] In 2017, 11 million deaths and 225 million disability-adjusted life-years were attributed to dietary factors, thus highlighting the need for improving diet globally. Low intake of grains, fruit and vegetables and high intake of salt were leading risk factors, along with saturated fats.

Is a plant-based diet the solution? Some commentators have said not. Chris Elliot of *The Independent* writes about 'hidden hunger'—the chronic lack of essential micronutrients in the diet, which over time can lead to severe health consequences.[29] It is, of course, for this reason that nutritional supplements and fortified foodstuffs have led to positive health outcomes in many contexts. Supplements are classed as food products, not medicines, by the European Union.[30] Under this classification, of course, they are *processed* foods, and as such, their manufacture and the resources consumed in their production must be factored into our thinking.[31] However, to an increasing extent, supplements are cited as having positive effects which address the shortfalls in modern diets.

The causes of hidden hunger are varied, but veganism, Elliot says, is likely to be a major factor. Poorly managed vegan diets, which do not replace the critical nutrients found in animal-based foods, result in problems such as iodine deficiency, reduced Omega-3 and B12 levels, and an increased risk of bone fractures.

For example, one study comparing fracture rates in four different groups (meat eaters, fish eaters, vegetarians and vegans) found that over an average of five years of follow up, the fracture rate was similar for all groups, except for vegans, who had slightly higher fracture rates, and a lower overall calcium intake. They concluded that an adequate intake of calcium was essential, irrespective of dietary preference.[32] Another study, however, suggests that slightly lower bone mineral density in vegans does not appear to be clinically significant.[33] In fact, vegans are not associated with an increased fracture risk if calcium intake is adequate. Plant-based foods can provide adequate key nutrients for optimal bone health.

But Elliot's warning is a helpful one. The consumption of cheaper, nutritionally poor, heavily processed food is of concern, particularly when suboptimal agricultural management and climate change have led to fewer micronutrients in our food. Poorly managed diets are not a problem unique to vegans. We all need the correct balance of vitamins, minerals and amino acids for our brain and metabolism to function.[34] However, few of us pay much attention to this.

Take the common scenario of, 'What shall we have for dinner tonight?' How often is the reply along the lines of, 'Well, I haven't had much zinc or protein today, so how about some cruciferous vegetables?' Our choices are often made along the lines of preference, habit and convenience, the more likely reply being, 'Ooh I know, we haven't had pizza for ages. I love pizza. Let's have that'; 'Good idea; shall we have it with some crisps and coke?' Biological, cultural and psychological factors determine the makeup of our diets. The food we buy, cook and share together is an important part of how we construct our personal and communal identity, with marketing playing a large role. How might we construct a Christian identity in our healthy food choices, and why might the vegan diet be a strong choice?

The Vegan Diet—A Strong Choice?

Research by the Oxford Food Programme indicates that a broadly healthy global diet could save five million lives per year; a vegetarian diet, seven million; but a vegan diet would have the greatest impact, at about eight million.[35] There is an increasingly strong body of evidence to support this:

- The World Health Organization has classified processed meat as a class–1 carcinogen, the same class as smoking, asbestos and radioactive barium.[36] All red meats have been classified as class 2 carcinogens, indicating that they are probably carcinogenic, based on evidence of links to colorectal cancer.[37] More detailed studies are indicating that risks of certain cancers are significantly lower in those who avoid animal products.[38, 39] These benefits are (generally) noticed where animal products are reduced to occasional consumption, but are greatest when they are eliminated; for example, specifically, veganism seems to protect against prostate cancer.[40]

- Animal products,[41] including white meats such as chicken, take much of their energy from saturated fat, which is associated with heart disease.[42] By contrast, those on a plant-based diet tend to have lower incidences of heart disease[43] and hypertension.[44] Plant sources of protein such as nuts and seeds have been shown to lower cholesterol.[45]

- Non-organic meat and dairy products contain hormones and antibiotics, given to livestock to increase rates of weight gain and feed efficiency. These have been linked with detrimental health outcomes.[46]

- Vegans have healthier gut profiles, with an increase in protective gut bacteria and a reduction in pathogenic types.[47]

- Vegetables and fruits contain a variety of nutrients, such as anti-oxidants, polyphenols, fibre, vitamins and minerals. It is therefore no surprise that increased consumption is associated with a reduced overall mortality risk from *any* cause.[48]

So current evidence suggests that in order to nourish and care for our bodies optimally, a plant-based diet is a prime option for consideration. As part of a careful and thoughtful approach to nutrition, the reduction of animal products in favour of plant ones, or the elimination of animal products altogether, does not lead to nutritional deficiency, but can provide extensive health benefits.

Questions for Reflection

- How much attention do I pay to the nutritional value of what I eat?

- What governs my food choices?

- What steps could I take to improve my diet and to either eliminate, or reduce those things which are not good for me?

4 Our Choices and the Earth—A Sustainable Option?[49]

Psalm 24 states that 'The earth is the Lord's and all that is in it;' he created it and 'saw that it was good' (Gen 1.24). Throughout Scripture we have glimpses of the earth's vocation, to reflect praise back to God and to be fruitful; for example, 'The meadows clothe themselves with flocks, the valleys deck themselves with grain, they shout and sing together for joy.' (Ps 65.13). The land is to be treated with respect, and not exploited to the point of depletion:

> For six years you shall sow your land and gather in its yield; but the seventh year you shall let it rest and lie fallow, so that the poor of your people may eat; and what they leave the wild animals may eat. You shall do the same with your vineyard, and with your olive orchard.
>
> (Exod 23.10–11)

In Genesis 4, we see the first act of worship in the Bible; Cain offers the fruits of the soil and Abel, the fat portions from some of his firstborn flocks, representing the inanimate and animate creation offered together. This is embodied powerfully in Holy Communion, when the bread and wine, 'fruit of human hands,' are used in worship of God. How we use the land, as workers or as consumers, is inevitably an act of worship.[50] Humanity's call to work the land implies this creativity and technology—the fashioning of the products of the earth for God's glory (Gen 2.15). Yet in employing technology and creativity, humanity often harms rather than enhances creation's ability to be fully itself, reflecting its praise back to God. As a result of the fall, the ground is now cursed, and working it is problematic for humanity (Gen 3.17). Our actions are often out of self-interest, rather than God's glory. The earth, along with its creaturely inhabitants, awaits liberation from its bondage to decay (Rom 8.21). So how might we best use the land to reflect our hope for this liberation?

Agriculture is a major stakeholder in the safeguarding of the environment. So in this chapter I examine the use of the land for food production through three lenses: greenhouse gases and other environmental pollutants; deforestation; and the over-use of land and water consumption.

Emissions and Pollutants

Emissions and pollutants are an almost inevitable part of technological advances, and the reduction of these is a major part of environmental efforts to resist global warming. The most significant anthropogenic greenhouse gases (GHGs) are methane, carbon dioxide and nitrous oxide, all three of which are produced as a result of meat production. The Oxford Martin Programme on the Future of Food has examined what impact emissions pricing would have on food.[51] Currently, GHGs from food production would make it very difficult to limit global warming to below two degrees Celsius. They estimate that if the cost of climate changes associated with GHGs were integrated into food costs, then beef would be forty per cent more expensive, and milk and other meats would cost twenty per cent more. This, conservatively, would lead to a ten per cent drop in the market for high-emission foods. Furthermore, they claim that if the world adopted a vegan diet, a scenario for ambitious mitigation, then it would cut GHGs by two thirds, and save £1.5 trillion in climate damages and health-related expenditure.

It is important, however, that a distinction is made between the effects of different GHGs.

Livestock is the single biggest source of methane. Past increases in methane emissions have caused warming as they occurred, but if the climate system is allowed to reach equilibrium with this level of methane emission (which takes about a decade), emissions at the same level will not cause further warming. The same can be said for nitrous oxide, which reaches equilibrium in about a century. Further increases will, of course, cause further warming. However, in the case of carbon dioxide, its effect on warming continues to grow as it is released. The cooling effect of reducing methane emissions compensates in part for delays in reducing carbon dioxide emissions, but net emissions of GHGs ultimately need to be reduced to zero to stabilize global temperatures. The reduction of meat production is therefore critical to the future of global warming.[52]

Livestock is the single biggest source of methane

Animal manure has been held responsible for excess nitrogen and phosphorus in surface and groundwater, thus harming both aquatic life and human health. However, this needs to be balanced with the use of animal manure as a substitute for artificial fertilisers, which require large amounts of energy to manufacture and therefore help to lower GHG emissions (although reducing GHG intensive meat production will be more efficient).[53]

Another concern is that of the use of non-renewable fossil energy to produce meat and dairy products. The lacto-ovo (milk and eggs) vegetarian diet uses half the energy, land and water resources of the meat-based—but neither diet is sustainable in the long term.[54]

The claim has been made that plant-based diets can produce more GHG emissions than meat or dairy per calorie.[55] However, according to *The Economist*, calorific calculations are outdated, as they do not account for nutritional value, nor for how different calories are metabolized.[56] In terms of GHGs and other pollutants, science seems to be encouraging a drastic reduction in the production of meat and dairy products.

Deforestation and Overuse of Land

> We currently devote seventy-eight per cent of all agricultural land to raising farmed animals, and feed more than one third of global cereal output to those animals. Philosophers and theologians from Plato onwards have noted that raising animals for meat is an inefficient use of land.[57]

One of the most significant ways in which humanity affects the environment is through the cutting down of forests to create pasture and for arable land to meet the demand for animal feed. According to the Union of Concerned Scientists, cattle play a significant role, using eighty-six per cent of the energy from agricultural land, but producing only eight per cent of the food we consume.[58] Over seventy per cent of the rainforest in South America has been cleared for ranching, and a further fourteen per cent for commercial crops, including soya for animal feed.[59] The market in soya exports is now one of the largest and increasing international commodity flows, with over half of the soy in the UK livestock sector feeding poultry. The resultant overgrazing affects biodiversity:

> These ecosystems would have been grazed by wild herbivores, but the much higher offtake from livestock changes and reduces plant species' diversity. The reduced plant cover and trampling on slopes leads to soil erosion and to further biodiversity loss. There has been considerable study of what combinations of wildlife and livestock densities best promote biodiversity in different ecological settings, and in some cases where native herbivores are no longer present, or extinct, livestock can help or be essential to maintain natural ecosystems. But in many developing countries, the understandable pressures from poor people needing to produce food lead to a vicious circle of unsustainable overgrazing and an increasing demand for grazing land.

Water Consumption

Agriculture uses more water than any other human activity, with almost a third required for livestock.[60] On average, beef uses more than three times as much water as chicken per kilogram of meat. This is mainly 'green water,' which falls directly onto the land. However, a significant proportion of water used is 'blue water,' from rivers and lakes, which competes directly with other needs, including that needed to maintain aquatic ecosystems. Water used to grow feed accounts for ninety-eight per cent of the total water footprint of livestock production.

Ambitious Mitigation?

Evidence seems to indicate clearly that significantly reducing global meat and dairy consumption would also reduce greenhouse gas emissions and other environmental pollutants, reduce deforestation and the overuse of land and enhance water security.

Although the livestock industry makes considerable demands on the environment, and most environmental research seems to promote an urgent reduction, there is an argument for retaining the industry in a lesser form. One study claims that land is used most efficiently if twelve per cent of dietary protein is derived from animals.[61] The role of animals here is to convert co-products from crop production into protein-rich meat and milk. Below twelve per cent, human-inedible products are wasted. Large populations, it is claimed, can only be sustained if animal products are used at this level.

What is clear is that our current dietary habits are not environmentally sustainable:

> Climate change cannot be sufficiently mitigated without dietary changes towards more plant-based diets. Adopting more plant-based 'flexitarian' diets globally could reduce the greenhouse gas emissions of the food system by more than half, and also reduce other environmental impacts, such as those from fertilizer application and the use of cropland and freshwater, by a tenth to a quarter.[62]

Dr Marco Springmann, from the Nuffield Department of Population Health at the University of Oxford, advocates a more ambitious mitigation (in that the severity of the problem warrants an ambitious solution), claiming that the vegan diet would have the greatest impact, cutting GHGs by two thirds and saving trillions of pounds in climate and health-related expenditure.

The gospel is an ambitious mitigation, as God in Christ reconciles all things to himself (2 Cor 5.18–20). As those entrusted with the message of reconciliation, Christians are called to ambitious mitigation against environmental brokenness. Moltmann states that if the universe is treated as a mechanism, within the control of human reason yet without reference to God, then our existence will be threatened.[63] As creatures who bear God's image and can know God's will, one legitimate means of ambitious reconciliation might be the adoption of the vegan diet, for the sake of the environment.

Questions for Reflection

- How much thought do I give to the environmental impact of my diet?

- What choices could I make to mitigate against the problems described?

- Am I open to considering the ambitious mitigation of the vegan diet, as an act of reconciliation?

Our Choices and the Global Population—An Equitable Option?

I have made the case that humanity's vocation to steward creation as an act of worship will involve attentiveness to the care of non-human creatures, ourselves, and the planet. I have offered evidence-based data to show that current levels of consumption are not sustainable in all three areas.

It is fair to say that, with the global population increasing rapidly, humanity has been rather successful at one part of our vocation as a species, to 'be fruitful and multiply, and fill the earth' (Gen 1.28). The second part of the command, to subdue the earth, is more complicated as demand for the earth's resources increase as a result. Sustainability implies current calculations of the projection of future need, so what might future needs in feeding the global population be?

Global Population Growth

The English clergyman Thomas Robert Malthus was influential in the disciplines of political economy and demography.[64] In his 'Essay on the Principle of Population' (1798), he observed that adequate food production improved the well-being of the population, but that this improvement was temporary because it led to an increase in the population, which restored the original *per capita* production level. Populations multiply geometrically (constant ratio growth), and food arithmetically (constant rate growth), so when food supply increases, the population will increase, thus eliminating the abundance, a phenomenon known as the 'Malthusian trap.' Populations tend to grow, he claimed, until the lower classes suffer hardship, want and greater susceptibility to famine and disease (Malthusian catastrophe).

When environmental and economic pressures rise, it is inevitably the poorest who suffer most. The poorest are hardest hit by the clearance of land for agriculture, and the most vulnerable, for example unskilled migrants, often end up working in the most difficult, dangerous and stressful jobs in the food industry. Given current global population projections, how might we avoid a Malthusian catastrophe?

Avoiding the Malthusian Catastrophe

Charles Godfray, Population Biologist at the University of Oxford, claims that demographic transition will reduce naturally in a non-coercive way.[65] As we bring people out of poverty and provide health care and education (especially for girls), population growth rates will plateau, at about eleven billion, by 2050. To provide for this increased population, we will need to produce more food. In the past we would find new continents or cut down forests, but now we need to produce more food from a smaller agricultural footprint. Godfray advocates the use of technology to increase productivity and resilience. Sustainable intensification is a goal, not a trajectory, and we can decide how to do this. His concerns are more about animal welfare than genetically modified crops, and he is optimistic about possibilities such as artificial meat, or alternative proteins.

The Potsdam Institute for Climate Impact Research estimates that food demand will double by from 2000 to 2050, thus forcing us to produce more crops to raise livestock than directly to nourish ourselves.[66] Population growth and Bennett's Law (that is, as wealth increases, so does the demand for refined grains, fruit, vegetables, meat and dairy) have led to estimates that demand for animal source protein will increase by seventy-two per cent between 2013 and 2050, thus requiring greater plant yields for feed and higher animal yields. The alternative, 'changing eating patterns and eating fewer or no livestock products, especially meat, is a possible solution to reduce the environmental impact' of animal agriculture and to reduce the *per capita* land requirements.'[67]

How likely is it that dietary modifications towards a plant-based diet will be sustainable? There is no single solution, and a number of strategies, combining dietary changes with technological advances and tackling food waste, must be employed.[68] The Institute of Physics (IOP) claims that currently, thirty-six per cent of the energy from the world's crops is being used for animal feed, and only twelve per cent of that energy ultimately contributes to the human diet, as meat and animal-based products. Notice the ratio here; only one third of the energy invested ends up feeding humans, thus losing two thirds of the potential food energy available. They claim:

> Given the current mix of crop uses, growing food exclusively for direct human consumption could, in principle, increase available food calories by as much as 70%, which could feed an additional 4 billion people (more than the projected 2–3 billion people arriving through population growth). Even small shifts in our allocation of crops to animal feed and biofuels could significantly increase global food availability, and could be an instrumental tool in meeting the challenges of ensuring global food security.[69]

They argue that global energy availability could be increased by as much as seventy per cent by shifting crops away from biofuel and animal feed, to prioritize human consumption. One limitation of their study, they concede, is that they treat plant and animal proteins equally when, in fact, plant-based proteins differ in their bio-availability. Animal products contain all essential amino acids, whereas plant-based ones only do so in combination. The mix of crops produced would realistically need to shift, for example, towards the production of more legumes. Future studies are needed to investigate how changing diets affect agricultural landscapes, including the use of land unsuited to crop growth. Arguments for both grazing livestock on such land and re-wilding such areas exist. As a result of expected changes in population and income levels, we may be approaching a situation which the IOP claim is 'beyond the planetary boundaries that define a safe operating space for humanity.'[70] Is a Malthusian catastrophe inevitable? Godfray is optimistic that technology can help—yet action will need to be taken both locally and globally to meet the challenge. The scientific community is agreed that one major means of addressing projected food requirements is to change our dietary habits towards a plant-based diet.

Changing behaviour is always challenging. People justify the consumption of meat on the basis that it is normal, necessary and nice, so the choice to consume it goes largely unexamined. Yet it is a huge injustice when what we consume has a serious impact on others. In 1978, Ron Sider claimed that it was clear that fewer people would go hungry and thirsty if more land (where possible) was used to grow crops directly for human food.[71] Scientific and technological advances seem to confirm this today. Our diets need to change in order to meet the demands of our own species, our fellow human beings. Meat and dairy consumption are ingrained into our habits. However, social norms and expectations do change, and can be aided by evidence-based education and the coordinated efforts of civil society, such as in the case of smoking cessation.[72]

Change for the Christian might also come through attentiveness to our vocation in our dietary habits, for the sake of others. God's care for creation extends to every single person on the planet. Revelation 7.9 speaks of 'a great multitude that no one could count, from every nation, from all tribes and peoples and languages, standing before the throne and before the Lamb.' All people matter to God, and deserve dignity and the opportunity to thrive. The Christian's vocation concerning our fellow human creatures is to ensure hunger, want and illness do not prevent this, and that our dietary choices align with this goal.

Questions for Reflection

- The global population currently stands at 7.7 billion. It is set to grow to 11 billion by 2050. How hopeful am I that technology can address the significant challenges for food production this will bring?

- Do I know what it is like to be hungry?

- What changes could I make to ensure that I contribute to others not going hungry?

6   The Plant–based Diet— A Viable Christian Option?

In this booklet I have argued that there are strong reasons for either eliminating or reducing our consumption of animal products on the basis of animal welfare, human health, environmental sustainability and the alleviation of global hunger.

However, a couple of significant matters arise which have not been addressed.

Matters of Culture and Economics

The EAT Lancet Commission recommends a 'universal healthy reference diet' consisting largely of plant-based food, with no or low quantities of red meat, processed foods, added sugar and refined grains.[73] They outline a hierarchy of policy levers, from the soft (education, incentives and disincentives), through to the hard (laws, fiscal measures, subsidies, penalties and trade reconfiguration). They claim that its adoption will provide positive outcomes for everyone by 2050 and beyond. They warn, however, that achieving this will require nothing less than a 'great food transformation'[74]

Gian Lorenzo Cornado, Italy's Ambassador to Geneva, is sceptical on cultural and economic grounds.[75] First, it would lead to the destruction of heathy traditional diets which are an important part of cultural heritage and social harmony in many nations. It is worth noting when discussing the concept of traditional diets that the traditional British 'meat and two veg' is, in fact, a relatively recent trend which has arisen since World War II rationing ended.

Secondly, the total, or nearly total, elimination of foods of animal origin would destroy cattle farming, and lead to the loss of millions of jobs, especially in developing countries. These are important considerations. However, the Lancet Commission's authors claim that adoption of the guidelines would vastly improve the health of most people on the planet, as currently hundreds of millions of people have insufficient food and many more consume low quality diets. They argue that flexibility to adapt local diets is built into the reference targets, as is the projected growth in demand for animal products in countries such as China. They also claim that fears of economic depression are unfounded, as targets for the developing world are balanced, for example, with *per capita* intake of meat remaining roughly at today's level across Africa. In other areas, farming will adapt as purchasing patterns begin to change.

The economic argument fails to convince, as consuming animals at current rates has been shown to be of detriment to human beings. A gradual reduction of global meat consumption would lead to food and water security, reduce environmental damage, improve health and reduce the risk of animal-borne human disease, all of which have strong economic benefits.

The Norwegian founder of 'deep ecology' Arne Naess, affirms this:

> Present assumptions about economics, development, and the place of human beings in the natural order must be re-evaluated. If we are to achieve ecological sustainability, nature can no longer be viewed only as a commodity; it must be seen as a partner and model in all human enterprise.[76]

It is noteworthy that in nineteenth-century Great Britain, Christians led efforts to question our assumptions about economics, development and humanity's response to our fellow creatures, for example through campaigning which led to the founding of the RSPCA. David Clough argues that there is a

> ...precedent, therefore, for Christians recognizing that their faith has implications for the treatment of animals and acting in response, and perhaps it is a timely moment for Christians to re-appropriate this as a faith issue, and recognize the implications for their own consumption, and for farming practice.[77]

The Matter of Scripture

For most of us, eating animal products is a very ordinary habit, and we do not link our food choices to our faith theoretically, nor practically to our ethical choices as disciples.

It is undeniable that the Bible does not prohibit the consumption of animal products and indeed, in some cases, it seems to advocate the eating of meat. It is true that in the creation narratives, humanity is given a purely plant-based diet (Gen 1.29).

It is also true that animal-based food was introduced after the flood (Gen 9.3). It is also true that Jesus seemed to follow an omnivorous diet, for example, eating fish (Luke 24.42). It is also true that Jesus 'declared all foods clean' (for example Mark 7.18–19).

It is true that that Peter's vision declares that God has made all animals clean (Acts 10.9–16), and that Paul seems to imply that only the weak worry about eating meat, and that eating or not eating it is irrelevant to our relationship with God (Rom 14.2, 1 Cor 8.4–8).

So it is possible to justify our consumption on the absence of a biblical mandate to refrain from animal products.

However, appealing to proof texts does not mean we can short-circuit Christian food ethics. New Testament questions are usually concerned with the choice to follow Jewish dietary laws, or the ethical issues around the consumption of meats offered to idols. They are not concerned with contemporary questions of food ethics.

The creation narratives suggest that one of the features of being made in the image of God is our agency. Scaer notes:

> Whatever the rest of creation does, it does because it must do it…[humanity] is not told 'you *must* eat' but 'you *may freely* eat.' [Humanity] can pick and choose.[78]

Indeed, it seems that as omnivores, we are not dependent only on plants or only on animals for survival. We are free to choose. Genesis 9 outlines God's covenant with all living creatures, and although meat is allowed, this is not indiscriminate, and an account is required for the lifeblood of creatures (v 5). We are accountable for the choices our freedom to choose affords. Through our calling in creation and through this covenant, we are accountable for animal welfare, for our own health, for the environment and for the well-being of others. We need to take this seriously, and recognise the contextual differences between contemporary agriculture and those encountered in Scripture.

Agriculture and farming in biblical times did not include the intensive raising of livestock. Ellen Davis argues that for the Levitical community, eating meat would not have been impersonal and private, as it is today.[79] Meat eating was tied up with sacrifice, and was therefore personal *and* public. Eating meat in biblical times was 'extraordinary, rather than ordinary.' If we stick to the freedom to eat what we like argument, then we fail to take into consideration the ethical implications of changes in contemporary farming practices, and in dietary habits and cultural norms.

Until recent decades, 'meat as a treat' would have been a common approach. Given the proven extraordinary demands animal products make on animals, the environment, and on human health, a return to extraordinary consumption—as encapsulated in the flexitarian diet—would be a positive step. A more radical solution would be to eliminate animal products from our diets altogether.

David Clough summarizes:

I appreciate that it is a big step to come to see what we have become accustomed to see as the ordinary act of eating animals as extraordinary, and to recognize that consuming the animal products of intensive farming may be in conflict with fundamental Christian beliefs about God's ways with creation. I submit, however, that careful consideration of Christian ethics in this area…requires nothing less.[80]

Questions for Reflection

- What do I think the Bible is saying about our choices and food?

- If I am accountable to God for the animal products I consume, how does this make me feel?

- What changes might I chose to make in my diet as a result of what I have read?

Diet	Meat:			Fish:			Dairy:			Eggs:			Plants:		
Vegan/Plant-based			N			N			N			N	H		
Lacto-ovovegetarian			N			N	H			H			H		
Lacto-vegetarian			N			N	H					N	H		
Ovo-vegetarian			N			N			N	H			H		
Flexitarian		O			O			O			O		H		
Western Animal Based	H			H			H			H				V	

Key: H = Habitual, O = Occasional, N = Never, V = Varied

Notes

1   The phrase 'plant-based diet' throughout this booklet refers to a diet which exclusively contains foods derived from plant sources, and eliminates all foods of animal origin. It is synonymous with the vegan diet, although veganism tends to have ideological and non-dietary connotations which are beyond the scope of this booklet.

2   https://www.bbc.co.uk/news/business-47480247

3   https://www.vegansociety.com/news/media/statistics

4   https://biblehub.com/interlinear/john/3-16.htm

5   https://biblehub.com/greek/3956.htm

6   G Tomlin, *The Widening Circle: Priesthood as God's Way of Blessing the World* (London: SPCK, 2014) p 74.

7   *ibid*, p 77.

8   K Vanhoozer in C Gunton (ed), *The Cambridge Companion to Christian Doctrine* (Cambridge University Press, 1997) p 166.

9   Tomlin, *op cit*, p 81.

10 Tomlin, *op cit*, p 74.

11 Tomlin, *op cit*, p 113.

12 D Clough, 'The Challenge of Christian Animal Ethics' 2019, https://www.youtube.com/watch?v=8MtsgHFLbF0&feature=youtu.be

13 D Clough, 'Consuming Animal Creatures: The Christian Ethics of Eating Animals,' *Studies in Christian Ethics* 30(1), 2017, p 38.

14 D Atkinson, D Field, A Holmes, O O'Donovan, *New Dictionary of Christian Ethics and Pastoral Theology* (Leicester: IVP, 1995).

15 Clough (2017), *op cit*, p 36.

16 D Migliore, *Faith Seeking Understanding* (Grand Rapids, MI: Eerdmans, 1991) pp 140–141.

17 Clough (2017), *op cit*, pp 32, 39–42.

18 Clough (2019).

19 M Dawkins, *Why Animals Matter: Consciousness, Animal Welfare, and Human Well-being* (Oxford University Press, 2012) p 173.

20 *ibid*, p 93.

21 Clough (2017), *op cit*, p 31.

22 D Ferguson, 'Creation' in Webster *et al*, *The Oxford Handbook of Systematic Theology* (Oxford University Press, 2007) p 85.

23 Dawkins, *op cit*, p 114.

24 https://www.nhs.uk/news/medication/antibiotic-use-in-farm-animals-threatens-human-health/

25 Dawkins, *op cit*, p 183.

26 Clough (2017), *op cit*, pp 41–42.

27 Clough (2017), *op cit*, p 44.

28 *The Lancet*, April 2019: https://doi.org/10.1016/S0140-6736(19)30041-8

29 C Elliot, 'Surge in the number of vegans is storing up health problems for the wealthy West,' *The Independent* (14 December 2018).

30 https://www.efsa.europa.eu/en/topics/topic/food-supplements

31 https://maddiet.co/why-mad-diet/

32 P Appleby, A Roddam, N Allen and T Key, *European Journal of Clinical Nutrition*, Vol 61, 2007, pp 1400–1406.

33 A M Mangels, 'Bone Nutrients for Vegetarians,' *The American Journal of Clinical Nutrition 100 (Suppl)*, July 2014, pp 469S–475S.

34 https://www.nhs.uk/live-well/eat-well/the-vegan-diet/ https://www.nhs.uk/conditions/pregnancy-and-baby/vegetarian-vegan-children/
35 M Springmann, H Charles, J Godfray, M Rayner and P Scarborough, 'Analysis and valuation of the health and climate change cobenefits of dietary change,' *Proceedings of the Natural Academy of Sciences USA* 113, 2016, pp 4146–4151.
36 WHO International Agency for Research on Cancer, 'Q&A on the carcinogenicity of the consumption of red meat and processed meat,' (2015): https://www.who.int/features/qa/cancer-red-meat/en/
37 International Agency for Research on Cancer Monograph Working Group, 'Carcinogenicity of consumption of red and processed meat,' *Lancet Oncology* 16, 2015, pp 1599–1600.
38 M Dinu, R Abbate, G Gensini, A Casini, F Sofi, 'Vegetarian, vegan, diets and multiple health outcomes: A systematic review with meta-analysis of observational studies,' *Critical Reviews in Food & Science Nutrition,* 57/17, 2017, pp 3640–3649.
39 T Key, P N Appleby, F L Crowe, K E Bradbury, J A Schmidt and R C Travis, 'Cancer in British vegetarians,' *The American Journal of Clinical Nutrition* Vol 100 supplement, June 2014, pp 378S–385S.
40 *The American Journal of Clinical Nutrition*, Vol 103, Issue 1, January 2016, pp 153–160.
41 L Hooper, N Martin, A Abdelhamid and G Smith, 'Reduction in saturated fat intake for cardiovascular disease,' *Cochrane Database of Systematic Reviews,* (6), 2015, CD011737.
42 Y Wang, C Lehane, K Ghebremeskel and M Crawford, 'Modern organic broiler chickens sold for human consumption provide more energy from fat than from protein,' *Public Health Nutrition* 13/3, 2010, pp 400–408.
43 Tao Huang, Bin Yang, Jusheng Zheng, Guipi Li, Mark Wahlqvist, Duo Li, 'Cardiovascular disease mortality and cancer incidence in vegetarians: a meta-analysis and systematic review,' *Annals of Nutrition and Metabolism* 60(4), 2012, pp 233–240.
44 Yoko Yokohama, Kunihiro Nishimura, N D Barnard, Misa Takegami, Makoto Watanabe, Akira Sekikawa, Tomonori Okamura and Yoshihiro Miyamoto, 'Vegetarian diets and blood pressure: a meta-analysis,' *JAMA Internal Medicine,* 174(4), 2014, pp 577–587.
45 L C Del Gobbo, M C Falk, R Feldman, K Lewis and D Mozaffarian, 'Effects of tree nuts on blood lipids, apolipoproteins, and blood pressure: systematic review, meta-analysis, and dose response of 61 controlled intervention trials,' *The American Journal of Clinical Nutrition* 102(6), 2015, pp 1347–1356.
46 S H Jeong, D Kang, M W Lim, C S Kang and H J Sung, 'Risk assessment of growth hormones and antimicrobial residues in meat,' *Toxicological Research* 26(4), 2010, pp 301–313.
47 M Glick-Bauer and M C Yeh, 'The health advantage of a vegan diet: Exploring the gut microbiota connection,' *Nutrients* 6(11), 2014, pp 4822–4838.
48 X Wang, Y Ouyang, J Liu, M Zhu, G Zhao, W Bao, F B Hu, 'Fruit and vegetable consumption and mortality from all causes, cardiovascular disease, and cancer: Systematic review and dose response meta-analysis of prospective cohort studies,' *British Medical Journal* 349/9, 2014, p 7969.
49 For specific discussion of environmental issues, see A Brown, *Changing the Climate* (Grove Education booklet eD24) and M J Hodson and M R Hodson, *An Introduction to Environmental Ethics* (Grove Ethics booklet E184).
50 G Tomlin, *The Widening Circle* (London: SPCK, 2014) p 82.
51 M Springmann, D Mason-D'Croz, S Robinson, K Wiebe, H C J Godfray, M Rayner and P Scarborough, 'Mitigation potential and global health impacts from emissions pricing of food commodities,' *Nature Climate Change* 7(1), 2016.

52 M Allen, M Cain, J Lynch, D Frame, 'Climate metrics for ruminant livestock,' *Oxford Martin Food Programme Briefing*, 2018.
53 H C J Godfray, P Aveyard, T Garnett, J W Hall, T J Key, J Lorimer, R T Pierrehumbert, P Scarborough, M Springmann and S A Jebb, 'Meat consumption, health, and the environment,' *Science* 361/6399, 2018.
54 D Pimentel and M Pimentel, 'Sustainability of meat-based and plant-based diets and the environment,' *American Journal of Clinical Nutrition* 78/3, 2003, pp 660S–663S.
55 M S Tom, P S Fischbeck and C T Hendrickson, 'Energy use, blue water footprint, and greenhouse gas emissions for current food consumption patterns and dietary recommendations in the US,' *Environment Systems and Decisions* 36/1, 2016, pp 92–103.
56 'Death of the Calorie,' *The Economist 1843*, April/May 2019.
57 D Clough, 'Consuming Animal Creatures: The Christian Ethics of Eating Animals,' *Studies in Christian Ethics* 30(1), 2017, pp 30–44.
58 https://www.ucsusa.org/
59 H C J Godfray *et al*, *op cit* (2018).
60 H C J Godfray *et al*, *op cit* (2018).
61 H R J Van Kernebeek, S J Oosting, M K Van Ittersum *et al*, *The International Journal of Life Cycle Assessment*, 21: 677, 2016: https://doi.org/10.1007/s11367-015-0923-6
62 M Springmann *et al*, *op cit* (2016).
63 Quoted in C Gunton, *op cit*, p 155.
64 P Millican, Hertford College, Oxford, 2017, PPE Lecture, 'General Philosophy: Matter, Mind and Humanity.'
65 https://www.oxfordmartin.ox.ac.uk/videos/view/720
66 P Pradhan, M K Ludeke, D E Reusser and J P Kropp, 'Embodied crop calories in animal products,' IOP Environmental Research Letters 8/4, 2013.
67 G Flachowsky, U Meyer and K H Sudekum, 'Land use for edible protein of animal origin—a review,' *Animals* 7/25, 2017.
68 M Springmann *et al*, 'Options for keeping the food system within environmental limits,' *Nature* 562, 2018.
69 E S Cassidy, P C West, J S Gerber and J A Foley, 'Redefining agricultural yields: from tonnes to people nourished per hectare,' *IOP Environmental Research Letters* 8/3, 2013.
70 M Springmann *et al*, *op cit* (2018).
71 D Clough, *op cit* (2017) p 33.
72 H C J Godfray *et al*, *op cit* (2018).
73 I Torjesen, *BMJ* 365/1700, 2019, pp 90–91.
74 *The Lancet*, 393/10170, 2019, front matter.
75 I Torjesen, *op cit* (2019) p 90.
76 http://www.deepecology.org/mission.htm
77 D Clough, *op cit* (2017) p 44.
78 D Scaer, 'Man Made in the Image of God and Its Relationship to the First Promise,' *Concordia Theological Quarterly* 41/3, 1977, p 24.
79 D Clough, *op cit* (2017) p 44.
80 D Clough, *op cit* (2017) p 44.